Historic Industrial Scenes:
SCOTLAND

A lobster fisherman with his gear on the beach at Birsay, in the north-western mainland of Orkney, about the turn of the century. Here is one of the celebrated 'fishermen with ploughs' described by the Orkney poet and writer, George Mackay Brown. This man was probably a part-time farmer as well as a fisher.

Historic Industrial Scenes

SCOTLAND

I. Donnachie, J. Hume & M. Moss

MOORLAND PUBLISHING COMPANY

To: The National Monuments Record of Scotland
In appreciation of their work
Si Monumentum require, circumspice

ISBN   0   903485   40   0

© I. Donnachie, J. R. Hume and M. S. Moss 1977

Printed in Great Britain by
Wood Mitchell & Co Ltd, Stoke-on-Trent

For the Publishers
Moorland Publishing Company
The Market Place, Hartington,
Buxton, Derbys, SK17 0AL

Contents

		page
Acknowledgements		5
Preface		6
Chapter One:	Rural Industries	7
Chapter Two:	Distilling and Brewing	19
Chapter Three:	Textiles	28
Chapter Four:	Mining and Quarrying	39
Chapter Five:	Fishing	52
Chapter Six:	Engineering and Iron Trades	64
Chapter Seven:	Shipping	78
Chapter Eight:	Inland Transport	89
Chapter Nine:	Other Industries	102
Bibliography		111
Index		112

Acknowledgements

In the compilation of this book the authors have incurred many debts of gratitude. In particular they would like to thank: Joan Auld, Dundee University Archivist; Kitty Cruft and the staff of the National Monuments Record; Richard Dell, Principal Archivist, Strathclyde Regional Archives; James Erskine, Paisley Museum and Art Gallery; Barbara Fairweather, the North Lorn Folk Museum; Alison Fraser, Orkney County Archivist; Peter Grant, City Librarian, Aberdeen; James Holloway, National Galleries of Scotland; A. S. Horsfall, Distillers Company Limited; Rollo Kyle, Scottish Design Centre; William Lind; Sir William Lithgow Bt; Jack Sanderson, Falkirk Museum; R. A. R. Smith, Transport Museum, Glasgow; Don Storer and Sara Crags, Royal Scottish Museum. The help of Miss Aileen Arnot and Mrs Rita Hemphill in the preparation of the typescript is gratefully acknowledged.

The authors and publishers are grateful for permission to reproduce photographs from the following collections: Aberdeen City Library for 3, 49, 50, 51, 64, 65, 67; Aimers, McLean & Co, Galashiels for 31 and 81; Ardbeg Distillery Co, Islay for 13, 17, 19; Bowie Castlebank Ltd for 115 and 124; Bridon Fibres and Plastics Ltd for 33, 37, 38 and 116; British Steel Corporation for 74; Carron Company for 69; the late Dr I. Cummings for 103; Distillers Company Limited for 16, 18, 20, 21, 22, 23; William Dobson (Edinburgh) Ltd for 125; Dundee University Archives for 35, 36, 40, 72, 79; Falkirk Museum for 27, 48, 100, 120, 121; Forfar Foundry Co for 10; Glasgow Art Gallery and Museums for 78; *The Glasgow Herald* for 71; University of Glasgow Archives for 96 and 109; Grangemouth Dockyard Co for 73; Inverness Museum for 77, 94, 105, 106; Sir William Lithgow Bt for 92; William Lind Esq for 41, 52, 53, 54, 55, 82, 85, 91, 107, 113, 114, 123; Mitchell Library, Glasgow for 42, 75, 119; National Galleries of Scotland for 29; National Monuments Record, Royal Commission on the Ancient and Historic Monuments of Scotland for 1, 9, 11, 14, 24, 58, 59, 61, 62, 63, 86, 87, 88, 93, 95, 97, 98; North Lorn Folk Museum for 56 and 57; Orkney County Archives for 2, 4, 5, 15, 28, *frontis*, 60; Paisley Museum and Art Gallery for 34, 101, 110; Parsons Peebles Ltd for 112; the late James Reid Esq for 6, 7, 8; Royal Scottish Museum, Edinburgh for 43, 45, 46, 47; Scottish Record Office and the Keeper of the Records of Scotland (British Rail Collection) for 83; Strathclyde Regional Archives for: 44 (Anderson Strathclyde Ltd), 66 (Pennycook Patent Glazing Co), 80 (Penman & Co), 84 and 90 (Clyde Port Authority), 99, 122, 126, 127; University of Strathclyde, Department of History for 70, 76, 104, 108.

Preface

Commentators on Scottish industry have naturally been pre-occupied with the basic industries — steel making, shipbuilding, heavy engineering, textile manufacture and coal mining — and have overlooked the many little industries vital to the well-being of the community. In the industrial centres these industries were dwarfed from the mid-nineteenth century by large concerns manufacturing products for world markets. In the countryside and smaller towns the separate character of these industries was preserved until the coming of cheap road transport and the development of synthetic materials. In the last twenty years Scotland's meal mills, malthouses, local breweries and distilleries, small textile mills and home spinners, quarries, little engineering works and iron foundries, rural railways, coastal and canal shipping, and such once familiar industries as paper-making, coal-gas manufacture and laundries, have all but disappeared or passed into the hands of large conglomerates. We are fortunate that in years gone by amateur and professional photographers turned aside from photographing outdoor scenes and wedding groups to record many of the once familiar crafts and industries of Scotland. In this book we have selected photographs mainly to illustrate the range of Scotland's smaller industries and to give a flavour of what it was like to live and work in the days before the motor car and the 'electric'. This provides a refreshing change from the ships, guns, locomotives, and boilers turned out by the great manufactories of West Central Scotland, which have been illustrated in *Clyde Shipbuilding from Old Photographs*, in the *Workshop of the British Empire* and in the *Glasgow As It Was* series.

I. Donnachie
J. R. Hume
M. S. Moss

Tulliemet: 1977

Rural Industries

Until recently most local communities — even the smallest — could boast a range of little businesses serving town or village and the surrounding countryside. A number of crafts and industries, particularly millwrighting, metal work, peat cutting, and the manufacture of bricks and tiles, developed to serve the needs of the farming community. Others, such as grain milling and timber sawing, processed the products of the land for a wider market.

Milling is the oldest rural industry. Following extensive agricultural improvement from the latter half of the eighteenth century, many new mills were built to grind increased quantities of grain. The most intensive period of mill-building in the Lowlands was between 1793 and 1815 when prices were inflated by the Revolutionary and Napoleonic Wars. Though water mills for grinding oats and barley continued to be built until the end of the nineteenth century, steam mills began to replace them as the century progressed. Rural mills declined rapidly after World War I except in more isolated districts. Drumtogle Mill (Plate 1) is a typical small country meal mill, with a kiln to the rear and a waterwheel on one gable. The Orkney wheel (Plate 2) is of the kind which could easily be assembled and maintained by local millwrights.

Windmills were far more frequently found in Scotland than might be imagined, especially in areas where water supply was erratic. There were once about a hundred windmills built mainly during the late eighteenth and early nineteenth centuries. Types were similar to those found in the north of England and Ulster. The most numerous were the familiar tower mills. The vaulted tower mill, which had a basement or cellar built into an artificial mound was peculiar to Scotland. The two windmills shown in Plates 4 and 5 were unusual even in their day.

Scottish millwrights (Plates 6 and 7) built many hundreds of corn and threshing mills. Although sometimes of a common design, each mill reflected the individual craftsmanship of the millwright. A number of types were built in different districts, the design adopted depended on the availability of water power, building materials and local demand. The distinctive flagstone and slate-built mills of Orkney and Caithness contrast with those further south in Fife and the Lothians, which were built of sandstone with pantiled roofs. The threshing mill was invented in Scotland in the late-eighteenth century and was rapidly adopted throughout Britain. Where possible mills were water powered, but in the fertile plains and on hill farms, horse engines were commonly used. In the East of Scotland the distinctive circular or polygonal houses were built in great numbers. Elsewhere the simple engines were normally in the open. With the development of the cheap and reliable steam engine, horse engines were gradually replaced by fixed or mobile engines. The portable threshing mills (Plate 8) were a familiar sight in the countryside until the advent of the combine harvester.

Timber cutting and sawmilling were of great significance in many parts of the countryside. Much Scottish timber was poor in quality and was of little use for building houses and factories — let alone ships. As a result most home grown timber was made into fencing stobs and pit props. In rural areas local-grown hardwoods, like oak, beech and elm were used to make waggons, furniture, buckets, clogs and coffins. Until the middle of the nineteenth century most timber was sawn into planks or baulks by hand in saw pits, but from about 1800 circular-saw mills driven by waterwheels were introduced (Plate 11). The steam engine was adopted in the larger, mainly urban, concerns from about 1850.

Peat is still the main fuel of the Western Highlands and Islands and is used widely in the malting of barley for malt whisky, giving it its distinctive smokey flavour (Plate 13). In Scotland most peat is cut by hand using traditional implements and spades which vary from one area to another.

Field drainage was necessary for the improvement of much farmland in Scotland. Stone-filled trenches were cut by hand until about 1850, when machinery was developed to make porous clay pipes (Plate 14). These were laid in trenches and covered in. Manuring the land was as important as drainage and in many areas near the sea, seaweed was used as a fertilizer (Plate 15).

The blacksmith (Plate 9) had an important role in the rural community. He made and mended farm machinery, horse shoes, household goods, gates and even simple bridges. In some of the larger market towns there were foundries employing several smiths and moulders. These concerns supplied waterwheels, waggon and coach parts and quite complex farm implements, such as potato lifters, seed drills, patent ploughs and hay turners.

Drumtogle Mill, ABERUTHVEN.

2   Miller and apprentice in somewhat uncertain pose atop a cast-iron segmental waterwheel in Orkney, about 1900. The retaining wall behind is built in flagstone, commonly found in both Orkney and Caithness (see also Plate 5).

1 Drumtogle Mill, Aberuthven, Perthshire during the inter-war years. The miller poses with his wares on the loading bay, while the farmer and his mate prepare to set off with the milk cart for local deliveries. The mill is a traditional two-storey and attic building with kiln behind, while the mill-wheel (apparently in motion) can be made out in the right foreground.

3

4

3 Maidencraig Mill near Aberdeen, photographed about 1890. The large wheel is the outstanding feature, while the kiln ventilator can be seen to the left of the mill range. The late James Reid, a north-country millwright, recalled working in this mill well before World War I: 'I remember a huge wheel and gearing at a burnt out mill near Aberdeen, 35ft diam. by 3ft 9ins wide, the buckets were all of cast iron and must have been a tremendous weight, as was the inside gearing'.

4 Peckhole windmill, North Ronaldsay, Orkney, about 1900. This turret postmill was built during the middle of the nineteenth century. It had four large sails which could be covered in canvas according to the strength of the wind. The rolled canvas is clearly visible on two of the sails. The mill was turned to take advantage of the wind by means of the large tailpole. Windmills were built in Orkney and elsewhere in Scotland where watermills were impracticable.

5 'Waiting for Wind, Orkney', about 1890. The crofter and his son have rigged the sails and are ready to go. This typical Orkney farm windmill was probably used to drive a set of millstones for grinding corn and perhaps a small threshing machine. The flagstone buildings, with turf and straw roofs are traditional to the islands (compare with Plate 2).

WAITING FOR WIND. ORKNEY.

6

7

6   The millwright's shop, Alness, Easter Ross, about 1920. This unusual photograph shows, standing on the right, James Reid, who was apprenticed as a millwright at the turn of the century. He built and repaired many mills during his career and had an unrivalled knowledge of mills in the North of Scotland. The portable steam engine was used to drive saws and other machinery.

7   Turning an axle-tree in the same millwright's shop at Alness about 1920. In this view James Reid, on the left, is removing bark using a two-handed turning tool. The oak axle would form the centre-piece of a waterwheel. Few new mills were built in the North of Scotland after the 1900s, and this was probably for a major repair to an existing plant.

8   Three newly-built portable threshing machines take to the road in Easter Ross in the mid-1920s. James Reid, who appeared in Plates 6 and 7, is standing in front of the traction engine wheel in the foreground. Threshing machines of this kind gradually replaced water- and horse-mills from the middle of the nineteenth century. In recent year they themselves have been eclipsed by the universal introduction of combine-harvesters. The traction engine here was built by Messrs Aveling and Porter of Rochester, Kent.

9

10

Saw Mill at Deans Haugh, near Elgin.

9 A farrier and his latest customer standing outside Causewayend Smithy, Kirriemuir, Angus, in the 1930s. The horse-shoe over the door leaves the casual observer with little doubt of the owner's occupation. Local smithies of this type were common in all localities until quite recently, serving the needs of the farming community. Horses were shod and machinery repaired at these smithies. Notice the usual jumble of iron around the smithy, and a grinding wheel in the right foreground.

10 A blacksmith at work in Forfar Foundry, Angus, in the 1950s. The smith is heating a workpiece in the forge prior to further hammering on the anvil at the bottom of the photograph. The heat of the fire is intensified by a blower at the bottom right-hand corner. The customary range of pincers and punchers is hanging on the wall behind.

11 Saw mill at Dean's Haugh, near Elgin, Morayshire, about 1856. This very early photograph shows a fine mill building with traditional East-coast pan-tile roof and crow-stepped gables. The cast-iron framed wheel with wooden paddles is undershot. The wooden building on the right houses the saw bench, which can be seen next to the door. Notice the bridge over the mill lade.

12 Making butter in a farmyard, probably about 1900. This carefully-posed photograph shows all the utensils required. The milk was placed in the tub under the table and allowed to stand until the cream had separated. The cream was skimmed off and put in the churn, on the left. Salt was added and the churn was rotated until the butter 'came'. The girl then made up the butter into pats and weighed it. This traditional rural craft is now extinct.

13 Distillery workers cutting peats for the Ardbeg Distillery, Islay, Argyll, (shown in Plates 17 and 19). In this photograph, taken at the turn of the century, the men are seen using traditional tools.

14 Making field drains at Blackpots brick and tile works, Whitehills, Banffshire in 1971. The workmen on the right prepare the clay, while the man in the centre loads it into the machine. The clay is extruded as a tube and cut into the required length by wires. A boy on the left lifts the pipes onto drying sacks prior to firing in a kiln. This interesting old works was in operation until recently.

13

14

15 Gathering in seaweed, at
Deerness, Orkney, about 1910. The
seaweed was either used as a
fertiliser or burnt to make kelp. Kelp
making was an important trade in
the Highlands and Islands at the
beginning of the nineteenth century,
but had virtually died out by the
time this photograph was taken.
Seaweed is still spread on the land as
a fertiliser in coastal districts.

Distilling and Brewing

From early times beer was brewed in private houses, educational and religious establishments, and 'small beer' was the most common beverage. The brewing industry began to grow from the middle of the eighteenth century when several notable firms were established in towns which subsequently became important centres of the trade. Early firms included William Younger of Edinburgh (whose brewery was located near the Royal Palace of Holyrood), James Aitken of Falkirk (Plates 25 and 27), George Younger of Alloa, and the brothers John and Robert Tennant of Wellpark Brewery, Glasgow. While large breweries serving urban markets were being established, smaller breweries were built in country towns, especially in the years 1780-1825. As beer was a costly commodity to transport, local breweries could survive and maintain business even in the face of competition from the bigger breweries in the cities. With the coming of the railways, Edinburgh became the brewing capital of Scotland with other centres in Alloa, Falkirk, Glasgow and Dundee. The country breweries declined. The only survivor is the Belhaven Brewery at Dunbar, East Lothian (Plate 24).

The history of distilling has been more romanticized than that of any other Scottish industry. Highland whisky was originally produced to alleviate the effects of the appalling climate and living conditions in the Highlands and Islands. A large proportion of the whisky produced about 1830 was illicitly distilled, as excise supervision in isolated straths and glens was difficult, if not impossible. Larger distilleries were established from the late eighteenth century. All the early distilleries produced malt whisky made from locally grown barley (Plates 16 to 19). After the 1820s grain whisky made from imported cereals (mainly maize) was distilled in the Lowlands. The mass-production of cheaper spirits led to the rise of blending in increasing quantities (Plate 21) — a technique of mixing different kinds of grain and malt whisky. Many of the most famous distillery companies started out as blenders. The pioneer blenders were Andrew Usher, established 1825; Alexander Walker of Kilmarnock, a licensed grocer who set up business about 1820 and introduced the long-lived 'Johnnie Walker'; and Arthur Bell & Sons, established in 1825.

16 A fine view of the Glentauchers-Glenlivet Distillery, probably photographed shortly after its opening in 1897-8. A typical courtyard arrangement of buildings includes the still house and kiln.

17 A malting floor at Ardbeg distillery, Islay, Argyll, about 1900. Maltsters, wearing clogs and using wooden shovels are stacking and turning the malt. The malt was made by spreading barley on a heated floor and leaving it to germinate for a few days. Wooden utensils were used to avoid damaging the grain. The germination process is arrested by drying in a kiln. Most malting is now done in large, continuous-process units.

18 The still house of the famous Talisker distillery, Isle of Skye. Here the excise officer is securing a pipe used to charge one of the four copper pot stills. This distillery makes a notable single-malt whisky.

19 Part of the still house in Ardbeg distillery about 1900. This view shows the padlocked tun where the spirit was stored immediately after distillation. On top of the tun is the spirit safe used for testing the specific gravity and hence the proof of the liquor.

20 Letterhead of the Cameron Bridge Distillery and Stores, Fife, of John Haig Sons and Company, taken from a bill made out in 1879 to David Russell Esq of Silverburn. The billhead cautions the recipient that 'Casks not returned within 3 months charged 2d per week till returned'. Notice the arrangement of buildings and railway sidings, and the small gas-works in the right foreground.

21 A blending room in the bonded warehouse of W. P. Lowrie and Company Ltd in Dunlop Street, Glasgow, underneath St Enoch Station, probably about 1880. Malt and grain whisky were mixed in these vats and married for a period prior to bottling.

19

22

23

24 Belhaven Brewery, Dunbar. Belhaven was established in the middle of the eighteenth century and is the last small-company brewery in Scotland. This recent view shows the brewhouse.

22 The cooperage of W. P. Lowrie and Company Ltd in Hydepark Street, Glasgow, about 1910, with casks in various stages of construction. The casks used for maturing Scotch whisky were generally old sherry or bourbon barrels. Cooperages like this were mainly involved in reconditioning them rather than in building from scratch.

23 Bottling and packing department of W. P. Lowrie and Company's blending plant at Washington Street, Glasgow, in 1907. Ranks of girls, wearing long aprons, are labelling, inspecting and wrapping the bottles, while men carry out the more arduous tasks of packing and stacking the crates.

25 The mashing stage at the Falkirk Brewery of James Aitken and Sons, about 1890. In the foreground is the mash tun being cleaned prior to mashing. The hopper above contains ground malt which will be mixed with hot water from the copper in the right background. Aitken's brewery, which was established in the mid-eighteenth century, was one of many to close in the 1950s and 1960s.

27 Bottling plant at the Falkirk Brewery of James Aitken and Sons, about 1930. Bottled beer increased greatly in popularity after the turn o the century and modernisation of bottling followed. Aitken produced highly regarded Pale Ales.

26 A nineteenth-century print showing the Candleriggs Brewery, Alloa. The town was one of the major centres of brewing in Scotland and this particular brewery was owned by the pioneering firm of George Younger & Son.

Textiles

The making of cloth is a complex process and has been carried on in Scotland from earliest times. The preparation of wool or flax, its spinning into yarn (Plate 28), its weaving, the 'finishing' of the cloth, and its making up into garments, were all carried out in the home until the seventeenth century. The first stage of the process to be mechanised was fulling (Plate 29) — or waulking, as it was known in Scotland. Development of cotton-preparation machinery from about 1765 led to the mechanisation of wool carding. Spinning and weaving remained hand operations until about 1800, when the first wool-spinning mills were built. In some of the Border towns hand-loom weavers were brought into workshops. The true factory-based woollen industry did not develop until after 1820. Small woollen mills were widely dispersed throughout Scotland, but there were important groups of larger mills in the Borders (Plate 31), the Hillfoot towns of Clackmannanshire and in Aberdeenshire.

After the Union of the Parliaments in 1707 the government encouraged the manufacture of linen in Scotland, particularly in the east. Linen was used to produce tablecloths, shirts, underwear, sailcloth, sacks and bags, and ropes. Because of the nature of the fibre mechanisation was slow. Flax plants were pulled whole — roots and all — and steeped in ponds. After some months the decomposed mass was dried and scutched or beaten to loosen the fibres. The fibres were then heckled (Plate 35) to comb out the shorter ones (or tow) and prepare the longer ones for spinning. Hand spinning and weaving of flax was more or less identical to woollen manufacture. Dundee and Angus specialised in coarse linen for bags and sacks. When a cheap new fibre — jute — appeared from India in the 1830s it was quickly adopted as a substitute (Plate 40). The Crimean and American Civil Wars stimulated the jute and linen industries. By the 1870s Dundee was the most important centre of jute manufacture in the world and was affectionately named 'Juteopolis'.

Rope-making was established in the seventeenth century as an accompaniment to shipbuilding and shipping. The major seaports all had their roperies. In 1711 the Gourock Ropework Company was established at Gourock. As shipbuilding on the Clyde developed 'The Gourock' grew and by the late-nineteenth century it was the largest firm in the world. Rope is made by spinning a coarse yarn and twisting a number of strands together to form twist. Three or more of these are twisted and laid in a ropewalk (Plates 36 and 37) in a 'house' machine (Plate 38) to form finished rope. The Gourock Ropework Company developed sailcloth weaving and sailmaking in parallel with its main activity.

Cotton manufacture was introduced in Scotland in the late 1770s. The attraction of cotton was the ease with which it could be spun mechanically. Large water-powered mills were built in most of Scotland's major cities. New Lanark was built on the Clyde by David Dale from 1784 and was extended by Robert Owen from 1800 to become one of the most celebrated mills. Woodside Mills on the river Don near Aberdeen is typical of the medium-sized cotton mills built from the 1780s. Steam-powered mills were later built in large numbers in and around Glasgow. Until the 1820s most of the yarn produced in these mills was exported or made into cloth by handloom weavers, mostly in their own homes.

From the mid-nineteenth century the traditional linen thread industry of Paisley (Plate 34) was eclipsed by the new cotton-thread trade. The invention of the sewing machine and its manufacture from the 1880s by the Singer Company in Glasgow stimulated demand and led to the emergence of J. & P. Coats as the largest makers of cotton thread in the world by 1900. This firm is still in business.

28 'At the spinning wheel, Orkney', about 1890. Spinning was a traditional country craft throughout Scotland and was carried out either as a profession or a hobby by people from all walks of life. It survived in country districts like Orkney until recently. The old lady here is wearing a machine-made dress, which certainly contrasts with the locally-made wooden clogs on her feet.

A Fulling Mill, Fife

29 A drawing of a fulling mill in Fife in the early eighteenth century, by Paul Sandby. This unique view shows fulling stocks driven by a waterwheel, but this arrangement of machinery in the open air seems rather unusual, as most 'wauk' or 'lint' mills were enclosed in buildings. On the left women are tramping clothes in tubs.

30 Woodside cotton mills, Aberdeen, shown in a fine drawing of about 1820. The Woodside Mills were built on the model of the Lowland cotton mills at New Lanark and Catrine. In the left background is Crombie's Grandholm woollen mill.

31　A weaving shed in a Border
tweed mill, probably in Galashiels
during the 1920s. On the right is a
hank-to-bobbin winding frame.
Notice the belt drives to the
machines from the roof.

32　A row of Jacquard looms in a
silk factory at Larkhall in
Lanarkshire about 1910. The
Jacquard apparatus above the looms
raises and lowers threads to form the
required patterns according to
information supplied by the punch
cards seen on the right.

33　Inspecting a net on the roof of
No 2 Mill at New Lanark, probably
during World War I. In the
background is the roof of No 1 Mill,
and on the right, part of Braxfield
Row, mill workers' housing built by
David Dale in the 1790s.

31

34

35

34 'With their flashy, dashy petticoats and flashy, dashy shawls', the girls from J. and J. Clark's Anchor Mills, Paisley, make a pretty picture about 1880. In the left background is part of the main mill block built 1871-5, and now demolished. To the right are piles of logs for the manufacture of spools.

36

35 and 36 Two photographs from James Banks and Son, rope and twine merchants, Perth, about 1910. Plate 35 shows a worker heckling sisal to tease out the fibres, while Plate 36 shows the start of the twine making process in the rope walk, with the traveller clearly visible. Compare the simplicity of this arrangement for making twine and light rope with the more complex equipment shown in Plate 37 for laying the heavier types of rope.

37

38

37 The rope walk at the Port Glasgow works of the Gourock Ropework Co Ltd, about 1910. This building was erected after the construction of the Glasgow, Paisley and Greenock Railway which runs in a cutting immediately to the right. Here on the left is the top cart with the traveller in front about to start forming a rope. The traveller twists the strands and the top cart lays the rope.

38 In contrast to Plate 37, this view shows a series of 'house machines' for making small-diameter ropes at the Port Glasgow works. These machines are situated in the floor above the rope-walk.

39 Tarpaulins and other canvas goods being manufactured at Port Glasgow about 1910. This particular building was originally designed as a sugar refinery in the 1860s.

40   Weaving shed of Baxter
Brothers linen and jute works,
Dundee in 1908. This photograph
shows the closely banked looms.
Notice that in contrast to Plate 31
the belt drive to the looms is from
beneath.

Mining and Quarrying

From the earliest times the rocks of Scotland have been quarried for building, monuments, and for civil engineering works. As towns and cities began to grow from the sixteenth century quarries for stone and slate became larger and more numerous. One of the earliest slate quarries was Camstraddan at Luss, on Loch Lomond, which provided the slates for the seventeenth-century Merchants House and the Old College of the University of Glasgow. In the nineteenth century, as slate displaced thatch, and the number of buildings constructed increased dramatically, new slate quarries were opened in Argyllshire, most notably on the islands of Luing, Seil and Easdale, and further north at Ballachulish (Plates 56, 57). The stones used for building varied from area to area. In central Scotland sandstones from the coal measures were quarried; in Caithness, Orkney and parts of Angus 'pavement' was used; and in Kirkcudbrightshire and Aberdeenshire granite was the chief building material. By the end of the nineteenth century the Aberdeen granite quarries were among the largest in Scotland and the Aberdeen granite works exported polished stone all over the world (Plates 49, 50). Some of the granite was used to make setts and kerbstones for urban streets, but the stone most generally used in the lowlands for road metal was whinstone, quarried from volcanic plugs, dykes and sills (Plates 52-55). In the Highlands small quarries were opened along the lines of the new roads built by General Wade and his successors.

Although coal was won from outcrops by mediaeval monks in the Lothians, it was not until the eighteenth century that coal mining became widespread. The growing demand for coal justified the large capital outlay involved, in the driving of drainage levels and the installation of Newcomen atmospheric steam-engines. After 1760, the expansion of the iron industry and, later the erection of steam-driven mills, encouraged landowners and merchants to sink new and larger pits. The industry flourished throughout the nineteenth century. Larger and deeper shafts were sunk (Plate 42), and the deeper workings required more support (Plates 43 and 45). The winning of coal was a hand craft until the 1870s when the first coal-cutting machines were introduced by the Bairds of Gartsherrie. Mechanical coal-cutting became popular when electric drive was perfected at about the turn of the century (Plate 44).

The expansion of iron smelting and working from the late-eighteenth century was only possible through the development of firebrick manufacture. The superior quality of the high-silica clays of the Glenboig and Bonnybridge areas in the central belt was discovered early on. Firebricks from these fields gained a world-wide reputation (Plate 48). Ironstone was mined in great quantity until the end of the nineteenth century, particularly in Ayrshire and Lanarkshire. Other metal ores were less widespread. Lead was mined mainly on a small scale, in several of the western counties. Leadhills and Wanlockhead were the most productive, while the Strontian mines gave their name to the element Strontium. Copper was uncommon, but in Renfrewshire and Ayrshire a few small pockets of ore were worked intermittently (Plate 41).

41

41 A classic industrial archaeology photograph showing the abandoned copper mine at Drumshantie in the hills above Greenock, Renfrewshire about 1890. In the foreground are the skeletal remains of a wood and iron waterwheel.

42 Carron Company's New Pit, Mavis Valley, Bishopbriggs, Lanarkshire in 1896. In this photograph a pit-sinking engine is being used to open the shaft, while in the background a new winding-engine house is under construction.

43 Loading coal from the navigation coal seam at Bowhill colliery, Fife, into a tub in 1906. Note the wooden pit-props — pit timber was a major import from the Baltic countries into the Forth ports.

44

45

44   A new type of electrically operated bar coal-cutting machine goes through its paces at Holytown Pit near Motherwell, Lanarkshire in 1903.

45   'Brushing' a road in Bowhill colliery, Fife in 1906. The roads in a colliery are the tunnels linking the working face with the pit bottom. Note that the rails on the left are of the bridge type, once common in coal mines. Old tram rails are in use as roof supports.

46   Coal-conveying machine at work near the coal face, Lady Victoria Colliery, Midlothian, 1926.

47 Winding engine and pit head, Lady Victoria Colliery, Midlothian, 1926.

48 Loading firebricks at G. R. Stein's works near Falkirk, 1930s. Until recently Scotland dominated the world market for refractory ware. Notice the counter-balance lifting bridge for crossing the siding.

49 A quarry near Aberdeen in about 1880. In the foreground is one of the first steam boring-machines used in a local granite quarry, while in the background stone dressers are at work on top of a recently loosened block of granite. The granite was split off the rock face with the aid of 'feathers' (wedges), the holes for which can be clearly seen along the side of the block. Note the foot-rest used by one of the dressers for working at the face.

48

49

50

51

50 Quarryman at Persley Quarry, Woodside, Aberdeen about 1920. He is dressing kerbstones. In the right background is a wooden Scotch Derrick-crane for raising stone from the quarry. Cranes of this type were developed in Glasgow in the mid-nineteenth century by the firm of Forrest and Barr.

51 Turning a block of granite in a stone-finishing works in Aberdeen about 1907. Notice the belt drive to the massive lathe, the very large spanners and the large pair of calipers. The workpiece is probably the base of a column.

52 A self-contained Baxter crushing and screening plant in the Craigenfeoch Quarry, Elderslie, Renfrewshire, about 1920. A traction engine is shown driving the plant via a belt, with the working face in the background.

53 Another view of Craigenfeoch
Quarry with horse-drawn carts
waiting to be loaded with screened
road-stone.

54 An early steam driller at work in the Craigenfeoch Quarry, preparing shotholes for blasting.

55 A Super Sentinel side and end tipping steam wagon owned by Gavin & Lind & Co Ltd, one of whose quarries features in Plates 52-54, in about 1920.

TELEPHONE
No 3, ELDERSLIE.

SPEED 20 M.P.H
C.W 6/12 0

No 5

WILLIAM LIND & CO LD
QUARRYMASTERS
&
CONTRACTORS.
ELDERSLIE

56 The slate quarry at East Laroch,
Ballachulish, Argyll about 1880, the
largest example in Scotland of the
type of terraced working common in
North Wales. Note the rope-worked
self-acting railway inclines, with one
of the winding drums in the
foreground. The boiler-house on the
left probably supplied steam for the
drills. The wagons are unusually
small.

Fishing

Fishing has always been an important source of food in Scotland. From mediaeval times fish were salted and dried to preserve them for eating during winter months and for export to the Continent. In the Highlands and Islands fishing was a seasonal activity which complemented the primitive agriculture of these regions. By the eighteenth century fishing had become important in the Forth and Clyde estuaries and along the East Coast, especially in the Moray Firth. From that time much was done to encourage the development of the industry by landowners, merchants and the Board of Trustees for Fisheries and Manufactures — a proto-Highlands and Islands Development Board. Similarly, the British Fisheries Society played a significant part in helping the industry in its formative years, establishing fishing harbours and planned villages in the North, notably at Tobermory, Ullapool and Pultneytown (now part of Wick). Fishing benefited from the tragic clearances of many parts of the Highlands, for some of the people were resettled on crofts near the sea and were expected to take up fishing to supplement their income. This transition has been poignantly described by Neil Gunn in his novel, the *Silver Darlings*.

Before mills, factories and some types of land improvement polluted the rivers of Scotland, salmon abounded and was a common dish in many households and religious communities. In the late-eighteenth century commercial salmon fishing was introduced on the principal rivers. The catch was par-boiled and packed in ice and sent to southern markets, particularly London. In the nineteenth century salmon fishing became the sport of the wealthy and landowners preserved their waters, limiting commercial fishing except on the Tay and Tweed. Coastal salmon and sea trout fishing continued and still survives, notably in Angus and Kincardineshire.

All round the coast of Scotland white fish (such as cod, haddock and flat fish) are plentiful. Originally they were caught on baited hooks strung together in thousands on linen lines. The women collected mussels, cockles and lug worms and baited the hooks and carried the men out to the boats so that they would begin their day dry. The men fished from open rowing or sailing boats all night. Initially most white fish were dried in the open air, but from the mid-nineteenth century railways allowed fresh fish to be distributed throughout Britain. However, drying continued in the remoter eastern counties and Orkney and Shetland for the export trade (Plate 68). From the 1880s steam vessels were used with drift or trawl nets. These boats were also used for herring fishing.

Herring fishing is a seasonal occupation as the herring is a migrating fish. Originally they were caught on lines, but during the eighteenth century sailing vessels were equipped with nets taking fish on a large scale. Most of the fish were salted (Plate 64) and occasionally kippered (Plate 67) as the oil in the flesh quickly goes rancid. Kippers were sold in the large towns and like the dried white fish exported mainly to northern Europe. As the herring industry grew, distinctive types of vessels emerged in all the main areas of Scotland (Plates 58-61, 63 and 65). The herring fleets moved round the coast of Britain during the season taking with them the fisher girls, who gutted the herring on the quayside. This seasonal employment was vital to many Highland families.

Both white fish and herring were sold round the fishing ports, usually by women or boys. The Newhaven and Fisherrow fishwives were legendary. Before the coming of the railway they ran with heavily loaded creels to Edinburgh to get the best prices, selling their fish from door to door (Plate 66). Fishing communities, even in towns, were self-contained and had their own customers. They were exceedingly devout, possibly because of the high risk of drowning. In common with other crafts and trades, fishing was an hereditary activity.

58 Herring boats at anchor in Vatersay harbour, Barra, Western Isles, about 1890. Boats registered in the East-coast ports of Wick and Inverness are tied up at the jetties in the foreground. On the quay are two long wooden troughs (similar to those shown in Plate 64) for use by fish gutters and cleaners, while the surrounding area provides storage space for a vast array of barrels and for fish nets. About 80 boats from Barra alone fished surrounding waters of the Minch at this period.

59 Nairn harbour on the Moray Firth during late Victorian times. The harbour was originally improved by Thomas Telford in 1820 and further extended following flood and storm damage in 1829. In this scene the masts of the local herring fleet appear in the background, while a trading bark *Bella of Findhorn* is tied up in the foreground. A complex of fish stores and curing sheds can be noticed immediately beyond the harbour, and the roofs and spires of the old town are just visible through the mist to the extreme right.

60 A momentary pause from the toil of fish packing at Stromness, Orkney, about the turn of the century. Members of the same family often worked side by side in this industry, and here is a typical family group with father standing in the background.

THE SEATOWN OF CULLEN, TIDE IN. 6243. G.W.W.

61

61 The Seatown of Cullen, Banffshire, photographed in the 1880s by George Washington Wilson. In 1885 nearly eighty fishing boats of the type shown in the harbour were based here. In the left foreground is a cooperage for the production of fish barrels; lengths of timber and partially completed barrels can be seen in the courtyard. Seatown or Fishertown is in the background. The traditional fisher folks' dwellings are built with gable ends to the shore, a feature common to many coastal villages of the North-East. Beyond the village is the eight-arched viaduct of the Great North of Scotland Railway carrying the line to Buckie, further to the west.

62 Fish landing and auction at Albert Quay, Aberdeen, at the turn of the century. When this photograph was taken steam trawling had already made considerable headway — the main catch being white fish. Typical trawlers can be seen at the quayside, while an auction proceeds in the right background.

63 Traditional two-masted 'scaffies' leaving Peterhead, Aberdeenshire, for the fishing ground, about 1885. The original caption reads 'Hoisting Sail'. Peterhead was one of the major centres of herring fishing and at this time had over 500 boats catching nearly 250,000 barrels of herring each year. During the herring fishing season the population of the town might increase by 3,000-4,000 persons, mainly employed in gutting and packing fish.

62

63

64   Girls gutting and packing
herrings at Aberdeen, about 1890.
The girls are ranged around a
wooden tub, similar to those
indicated in Plate 58. This
interesting photograph catches both
the camaraderie of the group and the
drudgery of its occupation.

65 The Aberdeen fleet puts to sea, 1883. This fine picture by George Washington Wilson shows 'Fifies' with full sail setting out for the herring fishing. In the background is the North Pier, started by John Smeaton in 1775 and later extended by Thomas Telford and others during the nineteenth century.

66 Newhaven fish wives at
Waverley Station, Edinburgh, about
1900. The fish wives often travelled
far and wide selling their wares, and
here we can see a group wearing
traditional frocks and cloaks and
surrounded by their creels. The
station is also seen to advantage in
this photograph, particularly the
carriage stance and booking halls.

67 Drying and smoking fish in
Aberdeen around the turn of the
century. Racks for drying fish appear
in the foreground, and beyond is a
range of curing sheds. Notice the
high ventilators or couls designed to
carry off smoke from the kilns.

68 Packing dried fish for export to
the Continent at Chalmers' fish
store, Kirkwall, Orkney, about 1900.
While the men bale and sack the
fish, the girl carries newly dried fish
from the curing house.

Engineering and Iron Trades

The iron industry in Scotland was on a domestic scale until 1605, when Sir George Hay built a blast furnace at Letterewe in Ross-shire. This remote location was chosen for the ready supply of coppice wood for making charcoal. Until 1760, the few blast furnaces were sited in similar areas, particularly Argyllshire. With the importation from England of coke smelting, the industry developed, slowly at first, but from 1830 with amazing rapidity. The Carron Company, founded in 1759, was the first large-scale ironworks in Scotland, making iron castings and a range of finished products including Newcomen and Symington steam engines and cannon. Although Carron was overtaken in output of iron by several other firms, it was not surpassed as an integrated ironworks (Plate 69). The largest single producer of pig iron in Scotland was William Baird and Co, with its associated Eglinton Iron Co. Its principal works were at Gartsherrie, Coatbridge (Plate 70). The foundation of Carron encouraged the growth of ironfounding in Scotland, which was further stimulated by the development or introduction of such new techniques as the cupola (for remelting scrap and pig iron), loam moulding, and later greensand moulding. 'Scotch Pig' was peculiarly suitable for the foundry, and Scottish moulders quickly earned a high reputation throughout the world for architectural and engineering castings (Plate 72). The greatest cast-iron building of all time, Sir Joseph Paxton's Crystal Palace was cast beside the Clyde at Renfrew by Fox, Henderson & Co. One of the main markets for heavy castings was shipbuilding and marine engineering (Plate 71). The growth of iron smelting and founding was paralleled by the rise of forging, initially of imported bar iron, but from the 1780s of home-produced iron. The larger engineering works and most shipyards had their own forges mainly for light work (Plate 73). Tubes were made from wrought iron from the mid-nineteenth century, and tubemaking became a West of Scotland speciality, particularly after steel was introduced in the 1870s (Plate 74).

The engineering industries grew out of ironfounding and forging. Until about 1850 most engineering works made a wide range of products, from grates to enormous low-pressure marine engines and locomotives. Marine engineering and locomotive building were the first specialised engineering products, and laid the foundation of the world-wide reputation of Glasgow as an engineering centre (Plate 75). From the beginning of railways, companies had their own workshops for repairing and later building locomotives and rolling stock (Plates 76, 77). Similarly the electric tramways installed in most of the larger Scottish towns and cities from 1898 were served by repair shops. In Edinburgh and Glasgow tram bodies were built on bought-in trucks, and the firm of Hurst Nelson of Motherwell gained a reputation as a builder of trams (Plate 78). Engineering flourished throughout Scotland (Plate 81). On the east coast, Dundee, Arbroath, Aberdeen, Leith and Kirkcaldy were notable centres (Plate 79). Boiler making was an important Scottish industry, serving the shipbuilding industry and the home market for land boilers (Plate 80). Civil engineering is often overlooked when considering engineering as an industry. During the nineteenth century Scottish civil and structural engineers had a world-wide reputation for designing and building railways, roads, dams, docks, harbours and lighthouses (Plates 82-84).

69 The newly completed blast-furnaces at Carron iron works, Stirlingshire near Falkirk, about 1890. This set of four hand-charged furnaces was one of the last of the type to be built in Scotland. The beds in the foreground were used for casting the iron into 'pigs' — bars of convenient size for manhandling. The tall cylinders on the flanks are Cowper Stoves used for heating the air blasts for the furnaces. These furnaces remained in use until 1963.

70

71

70 Preparing moulds for pig iron at Gartsherrie Ironworks, Coatbridge, Lanarkshire in 1933. The patterns for the moulds were designed to give a finished pig capable of being handled by a single man. In the background is the base of one of the blast furnaces, with the tap hole to the left of the second column from the left. The iron trough on the left carried slag to waiting tip wagons. The furnace is flanked by Cowper stoves for heating the blast air, using heat recovered from the blast-furnace gases.

71 The then new Clyde Foundry in Helen Street, Govan, Glasgow, of Harland and Wolff in 1920. This enormous works — the biggest foundry in the United Kingdom, was put up in anticipation of a post-war boom in ship construction. It was probably only fully used during World War II. The lorries in the foreground are carrying some of the foundry's products, including an engine bed-plate. The building was reckoned to be the largest glass-clad structure in the world.

72 The iron foundry of Douglas and Grant, engineers, Kirkcaldy, Fife in 1907. This photograph shows moulds in many stages of preparation. In the foreground can be seen the top and bottom of a big circular mould. Behind in the centre workmen are completing large moulds sunk in the floor. Note the overhead 25 ton crane and the smaller cranes along the wall.

73 The forge of the Greenock and Grangemouth Shipbuilding and Engineering Co at Greenock, Renfrewshire in 1910. A Rigby patent steam-hammer is at work in the middle of the forge, while the blacksmith on the left hammers out smaller components. Forges of this type are still a feature of Scottish engineering works.

74 Charging the tube furnace in No 1 Department of the British Tube Works, Coatbridge in the 1920s. Large diameter tubes of this type were made by pressure-welding two semi-circles of plate. After welding the tube was reheated and then rolled to a truly circular cross-section.

75 The Hydepark Locomotive Works, Glasgow, of Neilson and Co in the early 1860s. The building on the right is the original erecting shop which survived until the dismantling of the complex in the 1970s. One of the firm's own shunting locomotives can be seen below the water and clock tower.

73

76 The erecting shop of the North
British Railway at Cowlairs,
Glasgow, 1920. Some of the
locomotives are being built, whereas
others are in for repair. The
locomotive on the left is one of
Reid's Class S superheated 0-6-0
goods locomotives, the most
powerful freight locomotives
possessed by the railway, and on the
right is one of Holmes's 4-4-0
express passenger locomotives, by
that time used on secondary services.

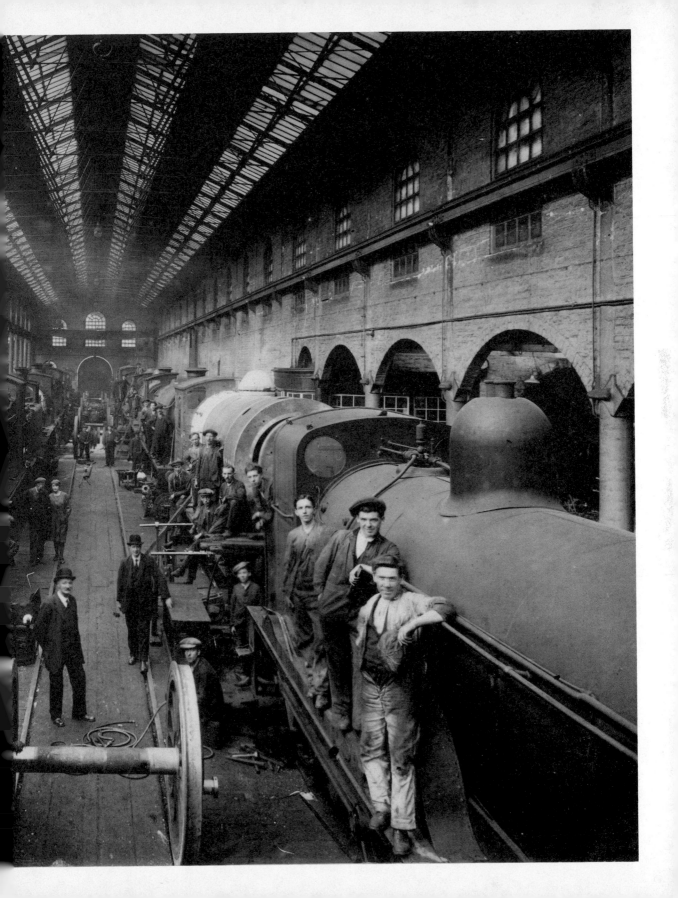

77   Breaking up locomotives at the
Lochgorm Works, Inverness of the
Highland Railway, about 1890. In
the days before oxy-acetylene cutting
was developed old rivets had to be
punched out by hand as is being
done in the background. An
impecunious company such as the
Highland Railway tended to re-use
parts of old engines. In the
background is one of the railway's
4-4-0 tank locomotives which
continued in service until the 1920s.

78 Building 'standard' tramcars in the Coplawhill works of the Glasgow Corporation Tramways Department in 1910. The trucks were brought in and the bodies built at Coplawhill. Bodies are being assembled on the left and in the background. These extensive works also overhauled the whole of the City's fleet of tramcars. These bays now house Strathclyde Regional Education Department's school bus garage, and the paint shop contains Glasgow District Council's fine Transport Museum, where two standard trams can be seen.

79 Erecting capstans and their driving gear during World War I at Douglas and Grant's engineering works, Kirkcaldy, Fife. In the background shells are being machined. Munitions of all kinds were made in every engineering works at that time.

80 Two traction engines hauling a large Lancashire boiler built by Penman and Co at their Caledonian Ironworks, Dalmarnock, about 1930.

81 A newly completed built-up pulley wheel in the works of Aimers, MacLean & Co, Galashiels, about 1920. Wheels of this type were used in rope drives for machinery, particularly in textile mills, and were made by general engineering firms.

84 An unusual view of the trench cut at Craigmaddie Reservoir, Milngavie, Dunbartonshire to be filled with puddle clay to prevent seepage of water from the reservoir. Note the railway line to carry spoil from the bottom of the trench. The Craigmaddie scheme was part of an extension of the Loch Katrine supply, completed in 1896.

82 The scale of nineteenth-century engineering works is not often appreciated. In this photograph navvies are excavating the interior of the James Watt Dock in Greenock, Renfrewshire, in the early 1880s. The dock entrance and one side wall can be seen on the right. The undertaking was completed in 1886. Note the mobile derrick cranes, a cumbersome but ingenious conversion of the Scotch derrick crane.

83 Excavating the south approach railway connecting the Forth Bridge with the Edinburgh-Glasgow line of the North British Railway in 1888. In the foreground is a water tank for the steam navvy. Note the horse and wagon waiting patiently for spoil.

Shipping

Communication in Scotland has until recently depended largely on ships. Trading between the east coast, England and Europe resulted in the early growth of ports such as Leith, Dundee, Aberdeen and Montrose (Plate 87). The coastal trades in coal, salt, corn, fish, and general cargoes were served by a large number of smaller harbours, which were improved from the seventeenth century — sometimes by local landowners (Plate 86). During the nineteenth century the advent of the steam ship caused a boom in harbour construction and extension, particularly for the coal trade and fishing (Plates 88, 89, 93 and 95).

The many natural harbours and sheltered beaches of the west coast were extensively used by fishermen and traders until the coming of reliable motor transport (Plate 94). The scenic attractions of the west Highlands made it worthwhile to run tourist services as far north as Fort William (Plate 96). As part of the 'Royal Route' from Glasgow to Oban passengers passed through the Crinan Canal (Plate 97). Likewise steamer services were provided on the Caledonian, and Forth and Clyde Canals until World War II (Plates 98 and 99). Only the Forth and Clyde, and Monkland canals ever carried substantial amounts of freight (Plate 100).

After the Union of the Parliaments in 1707, Scotland enjoyed the same trading privileges as England and a shipping industry quickly developed. By the early nineteenth century it had grown large. The dominant roles of the Clyde in perfecting the steamship and the skill of its ship designers in producing fast and economical sailing ships from the 1840s led to the founding by local men of a large number of well-known shipping lines such as the Anchor, Allan, Donaldson, Cunard, Burns, Lyle, Ben, Clan, and Elder-Dempster lines (Plates 91 and 92). Apart from the large shipyards on the major rivers, there were many small boatyards catering for the fishing and yachting communities (Plate 85).

85 Mr A. Smith posing in his workshop, probably in Gourock, at the turn of the century. As the board indicates he both built and repaired boats and yachts. In the background three boats have recently been completed, while on the left, the keel of a yacht is being made ready. In front of Mr Smith is a half-model of a yacht and on the left is an early marinised petrol engine. On his work bench to the far left is a hand-powered drilling machine.

86 Crail, Fife in the late nineteenth century. The harbour, still a popular subject for photographers, contains a ketch, the masts of which can be seen. The larger of the boats on the left are 'zulus', registered in Kirkcaldy. Behind them is Crail gasworks with the retort house in the background, and condensers to the right. The lean-to roofs presumably cover the gasholder and purifiers. Gasworks were sited as near sea level as possible to permit the maximum atmospheric pressure to act on the gas holder.

87 View of Montrose Harbour, Angus, taken in 1897, with two 'Old Salts' leaning in a characteristic pose on a hand-worked capstan. The vessel in the background has been drawn onto a patent slip for repair. The dock was built in 1843.

88 Leven Harbour, Fife about 1890, with a number of sailing and fishing vessels. Like Ardrossan, Leven was a coal port, but at that time, on a smaller scale. Here a line of wagons belonging to the Fife Coal Co, one of the largest Scottish mine owners, wait to be unloaded.

89 A woodcut of Granton Harbour and pier, Midlothian about 1880.

90

91

90 Ships berthed at Queen's Dock, Glasgow about 1890. In the background is the cone of the Verreville Glass Works and pottery and beside it the roof of the Scotia Engine Works which made steam steering-gear and other marine auxilliaries. The sailing vessels are typical of the steel-hulled ships being turned out by lower Clyde yards up to that date.

91 The crew of a sailing ship taken at Greenock in the 1890s.

92 The four-masted barque *Beechbank*, built by Russell & Co, Port Glasgow in 1892 for A. Weir & Co of Glasgow passing Greenock under tow. Many vessels of this type were built on the lower Clyde for Glasgow owners in the last twenty years of the nineteenth century.

93 The outer harbour, Ardrossan, Ayrshire, photographed by George Washington Wilson about 1890, showing a mixture of sailing ships and steam vessels. Ardrossan harbour was developed in the 1820s by the Earl of Eglinton as a competitor to ports on the upper Clyde. Notice the pile of pig iron stacked along the quay for shipment. In the background amongst the rigging of the two sailing ships can be seen a coal drop. By the late-nineteenth century Ardrossan was used largely for the export of coal, especially to Ireland.

94 A typical West Coast scene showing one of the celebrated Clyde puffers, probably about 1900. Cargoes were carried from the Clyde up the West Coast and the puffers ran aground at their destination to unload their wares. Goods were brought to the Highlands and Islands in this way until the improvement of road transport in recent times.

95 Camperdown Dock, Dundee, about 1880. In the foreground on the left is the mechanism for operating the lock gate. In the centre is the bow of a wooden paddle tug used for manoeuvring the sailing vessels.

96 The PS *Pioneer* off Staffa, probably in 1891. This vessel was built by Barr & McNab of Paisley for the Glasgow, Paisley and Greenock Railway in 1844. She was sold to David Hutcheson & Co in 1851 and lengthened in 1874, when the second funnel was added.

97 SS *Linnet* entering the bottom lock at Cairnbaan on the Crinan Canal, Argyllshire in the 1880s. This vessel was built in 1866 to replace horse-drawn track boats which acted as a link in the 'Royal Route' to the Isles operated by David Macbrayne. Passengers boarded the PS *Columba* or *Iona* at Glasgow, sailed to Ardrishaig, transferred to the *Linnet*, sailed to Crinan, and then took another Macbrayne boat to Oban. As she operated in fresh water the *Linnet's* engines were non-condensing. The *Linnet* only sailed during summer months and was laid up in a boat house at the top of these locks. This building still stands but is now roofless.

Inland Transport

Apart from the military road system created after the 1715 and 1745 Jacobite risings, the Forth and Clyde Canal was the first substantial investment in Scottish land transport. Although it was designed as a ship canal to link Glasgow with Europe and Leith with western Scotland and Ireland, it became a focus for industrial growth (Plates 99 and 100). The Crinan Canal was built from 1793 to 1801 to ease communication between Glasgow and Greenock and the western Highlands and Islands (Plate 97). Scotland's largest canal, the Caledonian, was constructed between 1803 and 1822 to create employment and to form a strategic link for smaller warships between the east and west coasts (Plate 98).

Railways were built to open up the rich mineral reserves in the central belt from 1823. They soon began to carry passengers and in the railway booms of the 1830s and '40s lines were built over much of Lowland Scotland (Plate 104). Carrying railways into the Highlands was an act of faith on the part of local landowners and merchants, though by careful management the Highland Railway achieved modest profitability in the face of extreme weather conditions (Plate 106). Under the Light Railways Act of 1896 it was possible to construct and work railways cheaply and there were many proposals to build light railways in the Highlands and Islands, mainly to facilitate the rapid transport of fish to southern markets (Plate 105). Another feature of late nineteenth-century railway investment was the improvement and extension of lines and buildings for growing traffic (Plate 107). Railways were also widely used in industry (Plates 108 and 109).

Street railways, or tramways were introduced in Glasgow in 1870 and built in several other Scottish towns and cities. Initially horse (Plate 110) or steam worked, most were converted to electric operation from 1898 (Plate 111) and many new lines were built (Plate 112). Tramways and railways supplemented horse-drawn transport. It is not generally recognised that the railways stimulated horse-hauled traffic in both town and country and later motor transport (Plates 114 and 115). This made a continuing programme of road improvement and maintenance all the more necessary (Plate 113).

98 A staircase of five locks at Fort Augustus, Invernesshire, on the Caledonian, Canal, taken in about 1890. A pleasure steamer is just leaving the top lock which still has its upper gates open. Note the hand-operated gear for the gate paddles and the capstan with their poles racked vertically to avoid accidents. In the foreground is one of the original cast-iron swing bridges, the only surviving example is at Moy near Gairlochy. The lock gates, then made of greenheart wood, are being replaced in steel.

99 The *May Queen* passing through Cadder bascule bridge, Lanarkshire, on the Forth and Clyde Canal on a dull summer week day between the wars. A passenger service was operated in the summer months from Port Dundas to Craigmairloch until 1939, by miniature excursion steamers. As with their counterparts on the Clyde estuary, a major attraction was the bar on board.

100 Basin of the Forth and Clyde Canal at Grangemouth, West Lothian, in the 1870s. In the left foreground are two coal barges, one with an engine, the other 'dumb'. At this time the canal was still regularly used for east-west traffic complementing the railways.

101 The Glasgow, Paisley and
Johnstone Canal at Saucelhill Bridge,
Paisley, about 1880. This view
looking west towards King Street,
(Saucel Street), shows the canal
shortly before closure. The sloping
bridge is typical of many built on the
canal. Framed in the bridge arch is
the wooden shed which formed part
of a small boatyard including a dry-
dock used for the maintenance of
canal barges. On the closure of the
canal in 1881, a railway was laid
along most of its length, though a
short stretch has been preserved in
the Ferguslie Mill complex.

103   Kincardine Bridge over the
River Forth, photographed by James
P. Cummings in 1937, a year after
its official opening. Prior to the
building of the Forth Road Bridge
linking Midlothian with Fife,
Kincardine provided the last bridge
before the estuary widens and was
therefore a vital link between the
eastern and western districts of
Scotland.

02   One of the 'wee ferries'
rovided by the Clyde Navigation
rust free of charge. No 1, built in
891 by D. M. Cumming at
lackhill on the Monkland Canal, is
een here in about 1910 approaching
he landing stage at Stag Lane,
ovan, on the Kelvinhaugh service.
he chimney in the background
erved the Kelvinhaugh refuse
estructor.

104

105

104 Scottish Central Railway 2-2-2
No 7 at Perth, with Alexander Allan,
its designer, wearing a 'gentle
shepherd' hat. The Scottish Central
Railway ran from near Coatbridge to
Perth, forming a vital link in the
chain of railway communication to
the North of Scotland. Note the
primitive leather buffers and chain
coupling. This photograph was
probably taken about 1850, making it
the oldest photograph in this book.

105 The Inaugral Train on the
Wick and Lybster Light Railway at
Wick station on 1 July 1903. The
0-4-4-T was renamed *Lybster* for
operating the branch line, which was
built to serve a number of fishing
villages.

106 A snow scene on the Highland
Railway at Inverness about 1890,
with the Ness viaduct and its signal
box. Underneath the box is a
horse-hauled wagon on the branch
from Inverness harbour.

106

107

107 A view of Gourock station, shortly after it was built in 1889. The Caledonian Railway constructed this magnificent terminus with its glass canopy and impressive range of waiting rooms to serve their steamers for piers 'Doon the Watter'.

108 One of the Glasgow Corporation's large fleet of narrow-gauge gas-works locomotives, Dawsholm Works No 6, built by Sharp, Stewart & Co, Atlas Works, Glasgow in 1893. This type of locomotive originated with Dugald Drummond, the well-known locomotive designer, in the period between leaving the Caledonian Railway and joining the London and South Western Railway, (see also Plate 109).

109 Piggy back for an 0-4-0 tank locomotive built in 1946 by Andrew Barclay Sons & Co, Kilmarnock, for the Provan Works of the Glasgow Corporation Gas Department. These small locomotives were used for working under the vertical retorts in all the Glasgow gas works. The last was withdrawn from service in the early 1960s. One is now preserved on the Welshpool and Llanfair Railway in Wales.

110

111

110 A Paisley horse-tram, probably towards the end of its days. The Paisley Tramways Company was incorporated in 1885 and had six cars, built by the Glasgow Tramway and Omnibus Co. The tramway was converted to electric traction by the Paisley District Tramways Co in 1903.

111 No 1 Tramcar of the Rothesay and Ettrick Bay Electric Railway about to leave Ettrick Bay in about 1910. The railway was built in 1882 as a horse tramway to carry tourists between Rothesay and Port Bannatyne and was extended to Ettrick Bay in 1905. It was converted to electric traction in 1902, when the tramcar seen in this view was built by Dick, Kerr & Co, of Preston.

112 Laying tram lines in Falkirk, 1901-2. The contractors were Bruce Peebles & Co, an Edinburgh firm of engineers who were pioneers of electrical engineering in Scotland. Although tram lines were put down in all the major Scottish towns during the Victorian era, photographs of the actual construction are very rare. The men on the left are using lifting gear to manoeuvre the heavy rails into position.

113

113   An outstanding photograph of
a road roller belonging to Malcolm
MacLean Niven of Crookston,
Renfrewshire, rolling a
'macadamised' road in Gourock in
1907.

114   Horse transport was still
important even in the Railway and
Tramway Age. This was particularly
true for short journeys in the town
and countryside. This photograph
shows an open landau outside the
Ashton Hotel in Gourock about
1900.

115   The first delivery cart of the
Kelvindale Laundry Co Ltd
photographed about the turn of the
century. This firm is now part of the
well-known Bowie-Castlebank
Group.

Other Industries

The wide range of crafts and industries necessary to support industrial and rural communities makes it impossible to group them all under convenient headings. This chapter draws together a catholic selection of common and unusual views — ranging from the rural crafts of Orkney chair making (Plates 117 and 118) through the handicraft of skip making in a factory setting (Plate 116), and the individual art of musical instrument making (Plate 119), to the manufacture of such necessities as paper and sweeties (Plates 120 and 122). The service industries of gas and electicity supply, and laundering are also represented in passing (Plates 123 and 127).

116 Making a wicker skip in Robert Owen's school at New Lanark in the 1950s. Sadly this ancient skill is now extinct in the West of Scotland, as the skips used in textile manufacture are made of sheet material.

117 A combing frame photographed in Orkney in about 1890. These frames were used to comb the ears out of the barley so that the whole length of the straw could be used for making panniers and Orkney chairs (Plate 118). Normal threshing damages the straw. This technique is still used in England for producing straw for thatching. Note the photographer's bag on the left.

118 Making an Orkney chair in about 1890. The woman is twisting twine from reeds, while the man builds up the chair back from bunches of straw. These chairs are highly prized possessions.

117

118

119 A remarkable view of the works of a musical instrument maker, probably in Springburn, Glasgow, about 1890.

120 The web end of Number 1 paper making machine in Carrongrove Paper Mills, Denny, Stirlingshire, about 1920. The pulp of fibres or 'stuff' flows into the box on the left through the pipes at the base, and out in a thick layer onto a moving belt of wire cloth. Water is drained away through the wire until at the far end the fragile still wet web is transferred to a woollen 'felt'. After squeezing to remove further moisture, the paper is dried on the bank of steam heated rollers in the background and is finally wound into a roll at the end of the machine (see Plate 121). This machine was made by James Bertram & Son, Leith Walk Foundry, Edinburgh.

121 Completing the dry end of a paper making machine in the same works as Plate 120 in 1909. In this machine the steam heated rollers are on the left and there are four sets of callandering rolls for finishing the paper after drying. The stand at the end is for the paper reels. This machine was built by James Bertram & Son of Edinburgh, one of the largest paper mill manufacturers in the United Kingdom.

122   Chocolate mills at Bailie
Agnew's Confectionary Works, Well
Street, Calton, in November 1917.

123   The Gourock Steam Laundry
with some of its staff at about the
turn of the century. Before the
widespread use of domestic washing
machines, laundries of this type were
common in nearly all Scottish towns.
The lettering on the box of the dray
on the right declares that the
telephone number of the company is
No. 1 Gourock.

124   W. & J. Bowie's patent carpet-
beating machine at work in the
firm's laundry, Dalmarnock in the
1950s. The introduction of carpet
shampoos and vacuum cleaners has
rendered this process obsolete.

122

123

124

125 Mechanical digger and men at work near Lady Victoria Colliery, Midlothian about 1930. The excavator was driven by a four cylinder petrol-paraffin engine and is seen here during the construction of a bridge over railway sidings adjoining the pit.

126 Bonnington Power Station, on the Falls of Clyde hydro-electric scheme completed in 1927 by the Clyde Valley Electrical Supply Company. This was the first major hydro-electric scheme in Scotland for public supply. Its effect on the spectacle of the famous Falls was much lamented at that time.

127   A hydraulic charging machine
for loading coal onto horizontal gas
retorts at Tradeston Gas Works,
Glasgow in the 1890s. Sir William
Arrol & Co, the Glasgow firm of
structural engineers supplied plants
of this type to many British and
overseas gas works from about that
time.

Bibliography

GENERAL

D. Bremner, *The Industries of Scotland: their Rise, Progress and Present Condition* (1869), new edition 1969, David & Charles

J. Butt, *The Industrial Archaeology of Scotland*, David & Charles, 1967

J. Butt and S. G. E. Lythe, *An Economic History of Scotland*, Blackie, 1975

J. Butt, I. Donnachie and J. Hume, *Industrial History: Scotland*, David & Charles, 1968

R. H. Campbell, *Scotland since 1707: the rise of an industrial society*, Blackwell, 1965

H. Hamilton, *An Economic History of Scotland in the Eighteenth Century*, Oxford, 1963

J. R. Hume, *The Industrial Archaeology of Scotland* (2 vols), Batsford, 1976-7

W. H. Marwick, *Scotland in Modern Times*, Frank Cass, 1964

R. N. Millman, *The Making of the Scottish Landscape*, Batsford, 1975

A. Slaven, *The Development of the West of Scotland*, Routledge & Kegan Paul, 1975

T. C. Smout, *A History of the Scottish People*, Collins, 1969

RURAL INDUSTRIES

I. Donnachie, *The Industrial Archaeology of Galloway*, David & Charles, 1971

A. Fenton, *Scottish Country Life*, John Donald, 1976

R. S. Morton, *Traditional Farm Architecture in Scotland*, Ramsay Head Press, 1976

BREWING AND DISTILLING

I. Donnachie, 'Sources of Capital and Capitalisation in the Scottish Brewing Industry', *Economic History Review*, 2nd Series, vol XXX, May 1977

P. Mathias, *The Brewing Industry in England 1700-1830*, Cambridge, 1959

R. J. S. McDowall, *The Whiskies of Scotland*, John Murray (2nd edition 1971)

R. B. Lockhart, *Scotch: the Whisky of Scotland in Fact and Story*, Putnam, 1974

TEXTILES

J. Butt (ed), *Robert Owen: Prince of Cotton Spinners*, David & Charles, 1971

C. Gulvin, *The Tweedmakers*, David & Charles, 1973

A. Thompson, *The Paper Industry in Scotland*, Scottish Academic Press, 1974

MINING AND QUARRYING

R. Page Arnot, *A History of the Scottish Miners*, Allen & Unwin, 1955

B. F. Duckham, *A History of the Scottish Coal Industry*, Vol 1 1700-1815, David & Charles, 1970

FISHING

P. Anson, *Fishing Boats and Fisher Folk on the East Coast of Scotland*, Dent, (new edition, 1974)

M. Gray, *The Highland Economy 1750-1850*, Oliver & Boyd, 1957

M. Gray, 'Organisation and Growth in the East Coast Herring Fishing, 1800-1855', in P. L. Payne (ed) *Studies in Scottish Business History*, Frank Cass, 1967

ENGINEERING AND IRON TRADES

R. H. Campbell, *Carron Company*, Oliver & Boyd, 1961

J. R. Hume, *The Industrial Archaeology of Glasgow*, Blackie, 1974

J. R. Hume and M. S. Moss, *Clyde Shipbuilding from Old Photographs*, Batsford, 1975

M. S. Moss and J. R. Hume, *Workshop of the British Empire*, Heinemann Educational Books, 1977

SHIPPING

B. Lenman, *From Esk to Tweed: harbours, ships and men of the East Coast of Scotland*, Blackie, 1975

G. Donaldson, *Northwards by Sea*, np, 1966

A. J. S. Paterson, *The Victorian Summer of the Clyde Steamers*, David & Charles, 1972

R. Simper, *Scottish Sail: A Forgotten Era*, David & Charles, 1974

INLAND TRANSPORT

I. Donnachie, *Roads and Canals 1700-1900*, Holmes Macdougall, 1977

A. R. B. Haldane, *The Drove Roads of Scotland*, Edinburgh University Press, 1968

A. R. B. Haldane, *New Ways Through the Glens*, Thomas Nelson, 1962

J. Lindsay, *The Canals of Scotland*, David & Charles, 1968

J. Thomas, *History of the Railways of Great Britain*, vol 6, Scotland, David & Charles, 1971

Index

Index of main places are indicated by
illustration numbers.

Aberdeen, 3, 30, 49-51, 62, 64, 65, 67
Aberuthven, Perths, 1
Alloa, 26
Alness, Rossshire, 6-8
Anchor Mills, Paisley, 34
Angus, 9, 10, 40, 87, 95
Ardbeg distillery, 13, 17, 19
Ardrossan, Ayrs, 93
Argyll, 13, 17, 19, 56, 57, 94, 97

Ballachulish, Argyll, 56, 57
Banffshire, 14, 16, 61
Barra, Isle of, 58
Belhaven brewery, Dunbar, 24
Birsay, Orkney, *frontis*
Bishopbriggs, Lanarks, 42
Bonnington power station, Lanarks,
    126
Bowhill colliery, Fife, 43, 45

Cadder, Lanarks, 99
Caithness, 105
Caledonian Canal, 98
Caledonian Railway, 107
Cameron Bridge Distillery, 20
Candleriggs brewery, Alloa, 26
Carron iron works, 69
Clyde foundry, Govan, 71
Clyde, River, 73, 82, 85, 90-3, 102,
    107, 126
Coatbridge, Lanarks, 70
Craigenfeoch quarry, Renfrews, 52,
    53-4
Crail, Fife, 86
Crinan Canal, 97
Cullen, Banffs, 61

Deerness, Orkney, 15
Denny, Stirlings, 120-1
Dunbar, 24
Dundee, 40, 95

Edinburgh, 66, 89
Elderslie, Renfrews, 52-4
Elgin, 11
Ettrick bay, Bute, 111

Falkirk, 25, 27, 48, 112
Falkirk brewery, 27
Falls of Clyde, 126
Fife, 20, 29, 43, 45, 72, 79, 86, 88
Forfar, 10
Fort Augustus, Inverness, 98
Forth Bridge, 83
Forth, River, 83, 86, 89, 103
Forth & Clyde Canal, 99, 100

Galashiels, 31, 81
Gartsherrie, Lanarks, 70
Glasgow, 21-3, 71, 75, 76, 78, 90, 102,
    108, 109, 115, 119, 122, 124, 127
Glasgow, Paisley & Greenock Railway,
    37
Glasgow, Paisley & Johnstone Canal,
    101
Gourock, 85, 107, 113, 114, 123
Grangemouth, 100
Granton harbour, Midlothian, 89
Great North of Scotland Railway, 61
Greenock, 41, 73, 82, 91, 92

Highland Railway, 77, 106
Holytown, Lanarks, 44

Inverness, 77, 106
Islay, Isle of, 13, 17, 19

James Watt Dock, Greenock, 82

Kincardine Bridge, 103
Kirkcaldy, 72, 79
Kirkwall, Orkney, 68
Kirriemuir, Angus, 9

Lady Victoria colliery, Midlothian,
    46, 47, 125

Lanarkshire, 32, 33, 42, 44, 70, 74,
    99, 126
Larkhall, Lanarks, 32
Leven harbour, Fife, 88

Midlothian, 46-7, 89, 125
Milngavie, Dunbartons, 84
Montrose, 87
Moray Firth, 59, 61, 63
Morayshire, 11
Motherwell, 44

Nairn, 59
Newhaven, Midlothian, 66
New Lanark mills, 33, 116
North British Railway, 66, 76, 83
North Ronaldsay, Orkney, 4

Orkney, *frontis*, 2, 4, 5, 15, 28, 60, 68,
    117, 118

Paisley, 34, 101, 110
Persley quarry, Aberdeens, 50
Perth, 35-6, 104
Perthshire, 1, 35-6, 104
Peterhead, 63
Port Glasgow, Renfrews, 37-9

Rossshire, 6-8
Rothesay, Bute, 111

Scottish Central Railway, 104
Skye, Isle of, 18
Staffa, Isle of, 96
Stromness, Orkney, 60

Tradeston gas works, 127

Vatersay, Barra, 58

Waverley Station, Edinburgh, 66
Whitehills, Banffs, 14
Wick, 105
Woodside mills, Aberdeen, 30